CRABS/ CANGREJOS

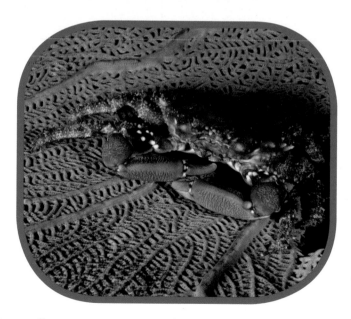

By Ryan Nagelhout   Traducción al español: Eduardo Alamán

Gareth Stevens
Publishing

Please visit our website, www.garethstevens.com. For a free color catalog of all our high-quality books, call toll free 1-800-542-2595 or fax 1-877-542-2596.

Library of Congress Cataloging-in-Publication Data

Nagelhout, Ryan.
[Crabs. English & Spanish]
Crabs − Cangrejos / Ryan Nagelhout.
    p. cm. — (Underwater world = El mundo submarino)
ISBN 978-1-4339-8780-9 (library binding)
1. Crabs—Juvenile literature. I. Title. II. Title: Cangrejos.
QL444.M33N33618 2013
595.3'86—dc23
                                        2012026204

First Edition

Published in 2013 by
Gareth Stevens Publishing
111 East 14th Street, Suite 349
New York, NY 10003

Copyright © 2013 Gareth Stevens Publishing

Editor: Ryan Nagelhout
Designer: Katelyn Londino
Spanish Translation: Eduardo Alamán

Photo credits: Cover, p. 1 © iStockphoto.com/Tammy616; p. 5 Colin Keates/Dorling Kindersley/Getty Images; pp. 7, 24 (shell) peter_krejzl/Shutterstock.com; pp. 9, 24 (claws) Jason Patrick Ross/Shutterstock.com; p. 11 © iStockphoto.com/tunart; p. 13 Photofish/Shutterstock.com; p. 15 Birute Vijeikiene/Shutterstock.com; p. 17 Ingram Publishing/Thinkstock.com; p. 19 CHRISTOPHE SIMON/AFP/Getty Images; p. 21 davidpstephens/Shutterstock.com; p. 23 MindStorm/Shutterstock.com; p. 24 (dinosaur) Hemera/Thinkstock.com.

Printed in the United States of America

CPSIA compliance information: Batch #CW13GS: For further information contact Gareth Stevens, New York, New York at 1-800-542-2595.

Contents

Old Animals 4

Claws and Legs 8

Kinds of Crabs 16

Words to Know 24

Index 24

Contenido

Viejos animales 4

Pinzas y patas 8

Tipos de cangrejos 16

Palabras que debes saber 24

Índice 24

Crabs once lived
with dinosaurs!

¡Los cangrejos vivieron
con los dinosaurios!

5

They have a hard skin.
This is called their shell.

Los cangrejos tienen
una cubierta dura.
Se le llama caparazón.

They often have
two sharp hands.
These are its claws.

Con frecuencia tienen
dos manos filosas.
Se les llama pinzas.

They have many legs.

También tienen
muchas patas.

Most crabs walk
side to side.
Others walk like us!

La mayoría de los
cangrejos caminan de
lado. ¡Otros caminan
como nosotros!

They will eat almost
anything small!
They eat plants
and animals.

¡Los cangrejos comen
cualquier alimento
pequeño! Comen
plantas y animales.

15

They come in many shapes and sizes. There are over 4,400 different kinds!

Los cangrejos tienen diferentes tamaños. ¡Hay más de 4,400 tipos de cangrejos!

They can live
in many places.

Los cangrejos pueden
vivir en muchos lugares.

Some are blue.
They can live in the sea.

Algunos son azules.
Pueden vivir en el mar.

Others are red.
They can live on land.

Otros son rojos.
Pueden vivir en
la tierra.

Words to Know / Palabras que debes saber

claws /
(las) pinzas

dinosaur /
(el) dinosaurio

shell /
(el) caparazón

Index / Índice

claws/(las) pinzas 8

kinds/(los) tipos 16

legs/(las) patas 10

shell/(el) caparazón 6

24

A ladybug is small and round.

Las mariquitas son pequeñas y redondas.

Contents

Meet the Ladybug 4

Flying High 10

Farm Friends 18

Words to Know 24

Index. 24

- -

Contenido

Conoce a la mariquita 4

Volando alto 10

Amigos de granja 18

Palabras que debes saber 24

Índice 24

Please visit our website, www.garethstevens.com. For a free color catalog of all our high-quality books, call toll free 1-800-542-2595 or fax 1-877-542-2596.

Library of Congress Cataloging-in-Publication Data

Appleby, Alex.
 [I see a ladybug. English & Spanish]
 I see a ladybug = Puedo ver una mariquita / Alex Appleby.
     p. cm. — (In my backyard = En mi jardín)
 ISBN 978-1-4339-8798-4 (library binding)
 1. Ladybugs–Juvenile literature. I. Title. II. Title: Puedo ver una mariquita.
 QL596.C65A6618 2013
 595.76'9—dc23

                                       2012022893

First Edition

Published in 2013 by
Gareth Stevens Publishing
111 East 14th Street, Suite 349
New York, NY 10003

Copyright © 2013 Gareth Stevens Publishing

Editor: Ryan Nagelhout
Designer: Katelyn Londino
Spanish Translation: Eduardo Alamán

Photo credits: Cover, p. 1 Vaclav Volrab/Shutterstock.com; p. 5 Ian Grainger/Shutterstock.com; pp. 7, 17, 21, 23 iStockphoto/Thinkstock.com; p. 9 Margo Sokolovskaya/Shutterstock.com; p. 11 Rudchenko Liliia/Shutterstock.com; pp. 13, 24 (wings) Symbiot/Shutterstock.com; p. 15 Hemera/Thinkstock.com; pp. 19, 24 (pests) forestpath/Shutterstock.com; p. 24 (trees) Comstock/Thinkstock.com.

Printed in the United States of America

CPSIA compliance information: Batch #CW13GS: For further information contact Gareth Stevens, New York, New York at 1-800-542-2595.

I SEE A LADYBUG/ PUEDO VER UNA MARIQUITA

By Alex Appleby

Traducción al español: Eduardo Alamán

Gareth Stevens
Publishing